WHSmith

National Test Practice Papers

English

Christine Moorcroft
and Ray Barker

**Age 13–14
Year 9**
Key Stage 3

The Publishers would like to thank the following for permission to reproduce copyright material:

Ian McEwan: from *The Daydreamer* (Jonathan Cape, 1994).
Purina Pet Care: from *Having Kittens?* booklet.
Lytton Strachey: 'Cat' from *Euphrosyne*. A Collection of Verse by Lytton Strachey et.al., (1905).

Every effort has been made to trace all copyright holders, but if any have been inadvertently overlooked the Publishers will be pleased to make the necessary arrangements at the first opportunity.

Hachette UK's policy is to use papers that are natural, renewable and recyclable products and made from wood grown in sustainable forests. The logging and manufacturing processes are expected to conform to the environmental regulations of the country of origin.

Orders: please contact Bookpoint Ltd, 130 Milton Park, Abingdon, Oxon OX14 4SB. Telephone: (44) 01235 827720. Fax: (44) 01235 400454. Lines are open 9.00a.m.–5.00p.m., Monday to Saturday, with a 24-hour message answering service. Visit our website at www.hoddereducation.co.uk.

© Christine Moorcroft and Ray Barker 2013
First published in 2008 exclusively for WHSmith by
Hodder Education
An Hachette UK Company
338 Euston Road
London NW1 3BH

This second edition first published in 2013 exclusively for WHSmith by Hodder Education.

Impression number   10 9 8 7 6 5 4 3 2 1
Year   2018 2017 2016 2015 2014 2013

Cover illustration by Oxford Designers and Illustrators Ltd
Typeset by DC Graphic Design Ltd, Swanley Village, Kent
Printed in Great Britain by Hobbs the Printers Ltd, Totton, Hampshire SO40 3WX

A catalogue record for this title is available from the British Library.

ISBN: 978 1444 189 346

NOTE: The tests, questions and advice in this book are not reproductions of the official test materials sent to schools. The official testing process is supported by guidance and training for teachers in setting and marking tests and interpreting the results. The results achieved in the tests in this book may not be the same as are achieved in the official tests.

Contents

The National Tests: A Summary

Since October 2008, secondary schools are no longer required by law to administer End of Key Stage 3 tests. The Department for Education requires all schools to report to them National Curriculum Teacher Assessment levels in English for all Year 9 students (Statutory Teacher Assessments – STA). These are also reported to parents.

At the end of Key Stages 2 and 3, teachers must use their knowledge of a pupil's work over time to make a teacher assessment judgement on a pupil's progress and performance across the key stage. This must take into account evidence of attainment in many contexts, including discussion and observation. A teacher assessment judgement must be made for all pupils, including those who are working below the level of the Key Stage 2 National Curriculum tests.

Optional tests, like the ones in this book, can help in that teacher judgement.

Key Stage	Year	Age by end of year	National Test
1 (KS1)	1	6	Phonics Screening Check
	2	7	KEY STAGE 1 – Teacher Assessment
2 (KS2)	3	8	Optional Year 3
	4	9	Optional Year 4
	5	10	Optional Year 5
	6	11	KEY STAGE 2 – Teacher Assessment
3 (KS3)	7	12	Optional Year 7
	8	13	Optional Year 8
	9	14	KEY STAGE 3 – Teacher Assessment

Levels

National average levels have been set for children's results in the National Tests. The levels are as follows:

LEVEL	AGE 7 (Key Stage 1)	AGE 11 (Key Stage 2)	AGE 14 (Key Stage 3)
8			
7			
6			
5			
4			
3			
2			
2a			
2b			
2c			
1			

■ BELOW EXPECTED LEVEL

■ EXPECTED LEVEL

■ ABOVE EXPECTED LEVEL

■ EXCEPTIONAL

What can parents do to help?

While it is never a good idea to encourage cramming, you can help your child to succeed by:

- Making sure he or she has enough food, sleep and leisure time during the test period.
- Practising important skills such as writing and reading stories, spelling and mental maths.
- Telling him or her what to expect in the test, such as important symbols and key words.
- Helping him or her to be comfortable in test conditions, including working within a time limit, reading questions carefully and understanding different ways of answering.

Testing at Key Stage 3

Optional tests are designed to help teachers raise standards by providing some extra evidence to support their own assessment. They can:

● help to identify a student's strengths and weaknesses

● help to provide extra support where needed – a case of 'assessment for learning'.

Optional tests at Key Stage 3 are designed for pupils working across Levels 3 to 7 of the National Curriculum for English. There are separate reading and writing tests, plus two Shakespeare papers (on each of two set plays) for Year 9.

Optional tests can be used during Key Stage 3 to:

● provide valuable diagnostic information about a student's strengths and weaknesses

● act as summative tests to produce a National Curriculum level.

Please note that teachers may choose to administer the tests alongside written work, class discussions and group activities and that tests are marked internally and results are not collected or published.

About the tests in this book

Tests in this book replicate the optional tests, i.e. you will find:

● English reading test stimulus materials – a variety of written passages on a theme and questions on those texts

● English writing test prompts – some issues to write about and help to structure ideas

● Shakespeare papers for *As You Like It* and *Romeo and Juliet*.

Paper	Time allowed	Content and marks	NC Levels assessed
Reading	75 minutes, including 15 minutes' reading time	Based upon three texts (32 marks)	Levels 4–7
Writing	75 minutes, including 15 minutes' planning time	Longer Writing Test (30 marks) Shorter Writing Test (20 marks)	Levels 4–7
Shakespeare	45 minutes	Reading and Understanding (18 marks)	Levels 4–7

No dictionaries, spell-checkers or thesauri are allowed in the optional tests for English.

The Reading Test

● This paper will include three texts. These will range across genres and can be literary, non-literary, fiction and non-fiction.

● They will be linked according to theme.

● The reading test lasts 60 minutes.

● Pupils will be given 15 minutes' reading time on top of this.

● There will be about 15 questions, which are varied in format.

● These will take into account pupils' different learning styles.

● Not all questions are of equal difficulty, but the mark scheme will be obvious.

The Writing Test

Writing ability is assessed using two written tests linked to the theme of the reading test:

1. A longer test (an open-ended piece). Pupils should spend a longer time on this question. It is worth 30 marks.
2. A shorter test (a more specific and succinct piece). Pupils should not write too much for this question. It is worth 20 marks.

The writing test lasts 60 minutes.
Pupils will be given 15 minutes' reading time on top of this.

Pupils will be required to complete both tests. The test will focus on:

● different purposes

● different forms of writing.

Planning formats will be provided in both cases.

Information is given about audience and purpose and usually about the form and the level of formality required in the writing. They will be marked according to three sets of criteria:

● sentence structure and punctuation

● text structure and organisation

● composition and effect.

The Shakespeare Test

The Shakespeare Test for Reading and Understanding will last 45 minutes. It is worth 18 marks. One question only will be set on each play. The question will test understanding of character, themes, language and dramatic conventions. The answer will be assessed only for understanding of the play and for how pupils respond to its literary merits. The test will concentrate on the detailed study of two sections of one of two designated Shakespeare plays for the year. The passages will be printed on the exam paper. For 2013 the designated plays are:

As You Like It
Romeo and Juliet

The set sections for the Year 9 optional English tests are:
- *As You Like It:* Act 1 Scene 1 (lines 1–55) and Act 2 Scene 3 (lines 1–68)
- *Romeo and Juliet:* Act 3 Scene 2 (lines 28–95) and Act 3 Scene 5 (lines 59–122)

There are two sections specified for each play and students should study both of the set sections.

Each paper (one for each of the two plays) contains a task based on two extracts drawn from one of the set sections. Each paper is based on one of the following four areas of assessment:
- text in performance
- character and motivation
- language of the text
- ideas, themes and issues.

Reading assessment focuses
Among the most important are:
- describe, select and retrieve information
- deduce, infer and interpret information
- comment on organisation and structure (including grammar and presentation)
- comment on a writer's use of language (including literary features at word and sentence level)
- comment on a writer's purpose and attitude and their effect on the reader
- relate texts to contexts, e.g. historical or cultural, as well as literary traditions.

Writing assessment focuses
Among the most important are:
- write imaginative, interesting texts
- write appropriately to topic, audience and purpose
- organise and structure texts appropriately
- write and construct coherent paragraphs
- write clear and varied sentences for effect
- write with technical accuracy, using appropriate grammar and punctuation
- select appropriate vocabulary
- spell words correctly.

Criteria for marking the writing tasks
- sentence structure and punctuation
- text structure and organisation
- composition and effect.

Tips for pupils
- Look at the entire test paper first to establish what has to be done. Highlight the time restraints and the number of questions which need to be answered.
- Which question is worth more marks? Spend more time on that question – but not too much more time. Write the times you need to spend on the questions by the side of them on the question paper.
- Keep an eye on the time! Look at how long you have to spend on this section. When you are practising questions, spend a little longer at first, but aim to become quicker. Remember: you will not be given any extra time in the real test! When they say 'put your pens down' – that's it!
- Read the questions carefully. Underline key words, e.g. 'compare', 'two reasons …'. Be relevant in your answers.
- Avoid getting too involved with any one question. You may have a great deal to say about it, but it will only be worth a set number of marks.
- Look at how many marks are allocated. Try to make that many points. If there are 8 marks, make 8 points (and back them up with proof). It won't be that easy really, but it will keep you looking for information and writing until the end.
- Follow the help given on the paper. If the examiners have given a list of points to follow then use these as the plan for your work.
- Make notes on the test paper. Underline important points, circle or highlight information relevant to the question. You have 15 minutes' reading time to start – no writing then – but you can start to get ideas and remember where key points are to be found. When you go back to underline things you will also be reading the text again. You only get the one chance so think about what you want to write before you put your pen to paper.
- Use quotations – but not huge chunks! You are using quotations to back up your points, not to fill up the answer booklet. It is best to quote short phrases and single words.
- If you get stuck on a question, leave it for the moment – but remember to leave a page empty in your answer book in case you want to go back.
- Your basic English is important – you need to communicate what you know and understand. Look carefully for those words you always spell incorrectly! Write in sentences and paragraphs – it makes your work easier to read. One rule should always be: Make life easy for the examiners!
- If you have time left, go back over your answers.

Advice for parents

Tests and exams can be very stressful. This is mostly because people do not like to feel 'judged' by others – especially if they feel that the results may not be as good as others expect.

The tests in this book are modelled as closely as possible on the 'real thing' so pupils will not be surprised by the test format. However, parents can help with the pressure of the tests by using the material in this book as a resource for teaching and learning. Do not just sit your child down with the test and tell him or her to 'get on with it'; share the experiences, questions and discussion that arise from the tests. Try sitting one yourself!

- Talk about each of the questions and possible ways forward. At this stage, discussion will be more useful than 'writing'.
- Choose a comfortable secure environment in which to do the tests together.
- Mark the work together, praising positive points as well as pointing out things which are not correct.
- Look closely at how the incorrect responses can be corrected, what needs to be learned or changed and how this can be done realistically. It is useful to list just two or three things which need to be done or learned before the next test session.
- Stick to the time limits – but do not insist that the entire test paper has to be completed at one go.
- Give immediate feedback – do not wait too long to discuss your child's performance.
- Be positive about achievements!
- Help your child to formulate specific questions for the teacher about any areas of difficulty.

How important are punctuation and grammar?

Punctuation and grammar are not assessed separately – there is not a fixed mark allocation for how an examiner feels you perform with these two key skills, although they are incorporated into the mark schemes. They are seen as integral to the communication of the ideas in the writing. You can know your subject perfectly, but if you cannot communicate what you know and understand clearly and effectively, then you are not showing yourself at your best. If you look at the criteria for marking on pages 32–34, you will find a useful checklist to help you assess your written work. You will be given good marks if your use of correct spelling and punctuation helps make your meaning clear; conversely, you can expect a less than favourable reaction if inaccuracy stops your reader understanding your work.

Test results

Page 42 shows how the marks for this test are correlated. However, the performance on any test in the book is only a guide. They do not guarantee the same result from the real thing! Remember … practice, practice and more practice! No one is motivated by being told they have 'failed'. Use the experience gained from this book to go on to improve performance.

- The paper is **1 hour 15 minutes** long.

- You have **15 minutes** to read the texts before answering the questions. During this time you should not start to write the answers.

- You then have **1 hour** to write your answers.

- Answer **ALL** the questions.

- There are 15 questions totalling 32 marks on this paper.

- Check your work carefully.

N.B.

Don't be afraid to underline or circle or highlight the key points in the texts as you are reading them. You can write in the margin of the booklets, too.

The theme of these three passages is 'cats'.

Read the following passage.

Then answer questions 1–5.

In this story, Peter swaps bodies with the family cat and experiences what life is like from the cat's point of view.

What a delight to walk on four soft white paws. He could see his whiskers springing out from the sides of his face, and he felt his tail curling behind him. His tread was light, and his fur was like the most comfortable of old woollen jumpers. As his pleasure in being a cat grew, his heart welled, and a tingling sensation deep in his throat became so strong that he could actually hear himself. Peter was purring. He was Peter Cat, and over there was William Boy …

That night Peter was too restless, too excited, too much of a cat to sleep. Towards ten o'clock he slipped through the cat flap. The freezing night air could not penetrate his thick fur coat. He padded soundlessly towards the garden wall. It towered above him, but one effortless, graceful leap and he was up, surveying his territory. How wonderful to see into dark corners, to feel every vibration of the night air on his whiskers, and to make himself invisible, when, at midnight, a fox came up the garden path to root amongst the dustbins. All around he was aware of other cats, some local, some from far away, going about their night-time business, travelling their routes. After the fox, a young tabby had tried to enter the garden. Peter warned him off with a hiss and a flick of his tail. He had purred inwardly as the young fellow squealed in astonishment and took flight.

Not long after that, while patrolling the high wall that rose above the greenhouse, he came face to face with another cat, a more dangerous intruder. It was completely black, which was why Peter had not seen it sooner. It was the tom from next door, a vigorous fellow almost twice his size, with a thick neck and long powerful legs. Without even thinking, Peter arched his back and upended his fur to make himself look big.

'Hey puss,' he hissed. 'This is my wall and you're on it.'

The black cat looked surprised. It smiled. 'So it was your wall once, Grandad. What'ya going to do about it now?'

'Beat it, before I throw you off.' Peter was amazed at how strongly he felt. This was his wall, his garden, and it was his job to keep unfriendly cats out.

The black cat smiled again, coldly. 'Listen, Grandad. It hasn't been your wall for a long time. I'm coming through. Out of my way or I'll rip your fur off.'

Peter stood his ground. 'Take another step, you walking flea circus, and I'll tie your whiskers around your neck.'

The black cat gave out a long, laughing wail of contempt. But it did not take another step. All around, local cats were appearing out of the darkness to watch. Peter heard their voices.

A fight?

A fight!

The old boy must be crazy!

He's seventeen if he's a day.

The black cat arched its powerful spine and howled again, a terrible rising note.

Peter tried to keep his voice calm, but his words came out in a hiss. 'You don't take ssshort cutsss here without asking me firssst.'

The black cat blinked. The muscles in its fat neck rippled as it shrieked its laugh that was also a war cry.

On the opposite wall, a moan of excitement ran through the crowd, which was still growing.

'Old Bill has flipped.'

'He's chosen the wrong cat to pick a fight with.'

'Listen, you toothless old sheep,' the black cat said through a hiss more penetrating than Peter's, 'I'm number one round here. Isn't that right?'

The black cat half turned to the crowd, which murmured its agreement. Peter thought the watching cats did not sound very enthusiastic.

'My advice to you,' the black cat went on, 'is to step aside. Or I'll spread your guts all over the lawn.'

Peter knew he had gone too far now to back down. He extended his claws to take a firm grip on the wall. 'You bloated rat! This is my wall d'you hear . . .'

Peter had an old cat's body, but he had a young boy's mind. He ducked and felt the paw and its vicious outstretched claws go singing through the air above his ears. He had time to see how the black cat was supported momentarily on only three legs. Immediately he sprang forward, and with his two front paws pushed the tom hard in the chest. It was not the kind of thing a cat does in a fight and the number one cat was taken by surprise. With a yelp of astonishment, he slipped and tottered backwards, tipped off the wall and fell head first through the roof of the greenhouse below. The icy night air was shattered by the crash and musical tinkle of broken glass and the earthier clatter of breaking flowerpots. Then there was silence. The hushed crowd of cats peered down from their wall. They heard a movement, then a groan. Then, just visible in the gloom was the shape of the black cat hobbling across the lawn. They heard it muttering.

'It's not fair. Claws and teeth, yes. But pushing like that. It just isn't fair.'

'Next time,' Peter called down, 'you just ask permission.'

The black cat did not reply, but something about its retreating, limping shape made it clear it had understood.

The next morning Peter lay on the shelf above the radiator with his head cushioned on one paw, while the other dangled loosely in the rising warmth. All about him was hurry and chaos. Kate could not find her satchel. The porridge was burned. Mr Fortune was in a bad mood because the coffee had run out and he needed three strong cups to start the day. The kitchen was a mess and the mess was covered in porridge smoke. And it was late late late!

Peter curled his tail around his back paws and tried not to purr too loudly. On the far side of the room was his old body with William Cat inside, and that body had to go to school. William Boy was looking confused. He had his coat on and he was ready to leave but he was wearing only one shoe. The other was nowhere to be found. 'Mum,' he kept bleating, 'where's my shoe?' But Mrs Fortune was in the hallway arguing with someone on the phone.

Peter Cat half closed his eyes. After his victory he was desperately tired. Soon the family would be gone. The house would fall silent. When the radiator had cooled, he would wander upstairs and find the most comfortable of the beds. For old time's sake he would choose his own.

The day passed just as he had hoped. Dozing, lapping a saucer of milk, dozing again, munching through some tinned cat food that really was not as bad as it smelled – rather like shepherd's pie without mashed potato. Then more dozing. Before he knew it, the sky outside was darkening and the children were home from school. William Boy looked worn out from a day of classroom and playground struggle. Boy-cat and cat-boy lay down together in front of the living-room fire. It was most odd, Peter Cat thought, to be stroked by a hand that only the day before had belonged to him.

The Daydreamer by Ian McEwan

Fiction Test Questions

Questions 1–5 are about *The Daydreamer*.

Use the space opposite to write your answers.

1. Explain how the cat solves the problem of the fight and why this was not seen as appropriate by the other animal.
In your answer you should comment on:
- what the problem is and how it emerges;
- how the characters deal with the confrontation in the early stages;
- the reactions of the other animals – and what they expect;
- how the boy deals with the fight.
Focus: Deduce, infer and interpret information and events or ideas from the text.

2. Show how the writer's use of speech enables him to characterise the cats.
Focus: Comment on the writer's use of language, grammatical and literary features (word and sentence level).

3. Find and quote three features which surprised Peter about being a cat.
Focus: Describe, select and retrieve information and events or ideas from the text. Use quotation and reference to the text.

4. Organise these stages in the cat fight so they are in the correct order. Write the correct letter in the appropriate box.
A. He rushed forward and pushed the black cat in the chest with his front two paws.
B. The black cat was balanced on the wall on three paws.
C. The black cat was caught off-guard by these tactics and fell backwards off the wall.
D. This was not how cats usually fought and so was unexpected.
E. He ducked and the black cat's paw missed him.

1	2	3	4	5

Focus: Comment on the structure and organisation of texts, grammatical and presentational features (text level).

5. Explain how the writer successfully creates the world of the cat for the reader.
In your answer you should concentrate on:
- what the character does and how he acts in his new life;
- how the author writes about the senses: what the character feels, sees, hears, etc;
- the reactions of the character in his new role;
- the way he describes these and his use of language.
Focus: Comment on the writer's use of language, grammatical and literary features (word and sentence level).

2

2

2

2

4

TOTAL

12

Read the pages from *Having Kittens?*, a booklet giving advice on what to do when you first get a kitten. Then answer questions 6–10.

Bringing a kitten home

Settling in your new arrival

Travel arrangements

When you bring a new kitten home, it is likely to be the first time he has spent apart from his mother and siblings, so he's bound to be a little nervous.

Do all you can to make your kitten comfortable by taking a proper cat basket with you: ideally one made of plastic-covered wire mesh, or wicker. If you don't have a basket, a large cardboard box will do, providing it has good ventilation and is secure. Add some soft bedding (an old blanket or towel is ideal), and don't be surprised if your kitten soils it on the way home.

During the journey, you may like to talk to your kitten. The sound of your voice will help to reassure him – and become a familiar comfort in the days ahead.

Exploring new territory

It's a good idea to pre-prepare a place for your kitten: somewhere reasonably quiet, free of dangers (such as open windows), and clear of valuables. As you will discover, kittens and breakable objects tend to find each other fast!

Let your kitten explore his new surroundings at his own pace. He will probably sleep A LOT – up to 20 hours a day is normal (even adult cats sleep an average of 16 hours a day).

If your kitten won't bed down in the place you have prepared for him, it's probably easiest to let him have his own way – by moving the bed to the kitten. Remember to place his feeding bowl, water and litter tray within easy reach.

Getting better acquainted

Once your kitten has settled in, he'll start to enjoy the affection you show him, so pick him up and talk to him.

If you have children, explain that your kitten is not a toy. They must be gentle and kind when handling him – and you must all be prepared for the odd nip or playful claw as your kitten gets used to you.

If you have other pets, introduce your kitten slowly. If in any doubt, keep your kitten in his carry basket around larger animals and do not leave him unattended. In time, they should become friends – or at least tolerant housemates!

Paws for thought:
- Your kitten will sleep for up to 20 hours a day
- Allow him to explore at his own pace
- Supervise your kitten around children and larger pets

The good kitten guide

Keeping mischief to a minimum

Basic 'do's and 'don't's

The sooner you start getting your message across, the sooner your kitten will understand what is, and is not, acceptable behaviour. As a guide:

Do use his name, or make a particular sound, which your kitten can associate with feeding and play time.

Don't be too harsh when your new kitten makes mistakes. As an instinctive hunter, he will naturally try his claws out on your furniture and curtains.

Do encourage appropriate scratching behaviour and place him by his scratching post, so he can see where it's OK to sharpen his claws.

Don't slap or strike your cat. If you need to discipline him, a loud clap of the hands and a firm 'no' will do.

Do show him affection. Once he trusts you, he will start to respect you – a little bit, at least!

Do be aware that accidents can happen. Some plants are poisonous to cats – contact your vet if concerned.

Toilet training

Until your kitten has had his course of vaccinations he will need to use a litter tray. You can fill it with earth or sand, but commercially available cat litter is probably easier – and less smelly.

The best way to encourage your kitten to use his litter tray is to put it in a private but easily accessible location. Place him gently inside it immediately after every meal – and whenever you see him crouching down as if to relieve himself. And make a fuss of him whenever he has used it successfully.

It is also a good idea to invest in a plastic 'pooper scooper' to get rid of any mess immediately. And litter should be completely renewed every two or three days.

Safety first

Always wear rubber gloves when you're cleaning the litter tray, and wash your hands thoroughly afterwards. Pregnant women should be especially careful: if possible, get someone else to perform 'toilet duty' for a while.

From *Having Kittens?*

Non-Fiction Test Questions

Questions 6–10 are about Having Kittens?

Use the space below and opposite to write your answers.

6. Quote one good reason why you should bring a plastic-covered wire mesh or wicker basket to pick up your kitten.
Focus: Describe, select and retrieve information and events or ideas from the text. Use quotation and reference to the text.

1

7. Describe two dangers of which an owner needs to be aware when he or she first allows the kitten to explore its new environment.
Focus: Describe, select and retrieve information and events or ideas from the text. Use quotation and reference to the text.

2

8. Explain why:
a) you need to make a particular sound or use a name when talking to your new pet.
b) you should place the kitten *gently* in his litter tray after every meal.
Focus: Deduce, infer and interpret information and events or ideas from the text.

2

9. Identify some of the stylistic features of this booklet which suggest it is giving instructions.
Focus: Comment on the writer's use of language, grammatical and literary features (word and sentence level).

2

10. This booklet is given to people who become owners of a kitten for the first time. How effective do you think the pages from this booklet are in getting the messages across simply and clearly?
In your answer you should comment on:
- the language which is used to suit the reader;
- the way language is used to inform and influence the reader;
- the layout of the leaflet;
- the way it makes an emotional appeal.
Focus: Identify and comment on the writer's purposes and viewpoints and the effect of the text on the reader.

5

_____

_____

_____

TOTAL

_____

_____

12

Dear creature by the fire a-purr,
Strange idol, eminently bland,
Miraculous puss! As o'er your fur
I trail a negligible hand,

And gaze into your gazing eyes,
And wonder in a demi-dream,
What mystery it is that lies,
Behind those slits that glare and gleam,

An exquisite enchantment falls
About the portals of my sense;
Meandering through enormous halls,
I breathe luxurious frankincense,

An ampler air, a warmer June
Enfold me, and my wondering eye
Salutes a more imperial moon
Throned in a more resplendent sky

Than ever knew this northern shore.
Oh, strange! For you are with me too,
And I who am a cat once more
Follow the woman that was you

With tail erect and pompous march,
The proudest puss that ever trod,
Through many a grove, 'neath many an arch,
Impenetrable as a god.

Down many an alabaster flight
Of broad and cedar-shaded stairs,
While over us the elaborate night
Mysteriously gleams and glares.

From *Cat* by Lytton Strachey

Poetry Test Questions

Questions 11–15 are about *Cat.*

Write your answers on a separate sheet of paper.

11. Find and quote the words used in the poem to suggest that this is not a modern poem.
Focus: Describe, select and retrieve information and events or ideas from the text. Use quotation and reference to the text.

1

12. Quote two adjectives used in the third and fourth verses which suggest that the cat is from a royal background.
Focus: Comment on the writer's use of language, grammatical and literary features (word and sentence level).

1

13. Explain why the cat is:
With tail erect and pompous march,
The proudest puss that ever trod,
and show what picture the writer has created of the cat by using these adjectives.
Focus: Deduce, infer and interpret information and events or ideas from the text.

2

14. Comment on the picture created by the metaphor:
my wondering eye
Salutes a more imperial moon
Throned in a more resplendent sky.
Focus: Comment on the writer's use of language, grammatical and literary features (word and sentence level).

2

15. Match the correct verse to its subject by drawing a line between the two boxes.

Verse	Subject
1	The poet wonders what mystery lies behind the eyes of the cat.
2	The poet feels he is in a warmer place with an exotic moon.
3	The poet strokes the cat as she sleeps.
4	The cat is proud and honoured in this society.
5	The poet suddenly feels as if he has been transported to an ancient time with incense and palaces.
6	The poet imagines the cat in an ancient palace at night.
7	The poet feels he is the cat following a woman in ancient times.

2

Focus: Comment on the structure and organisation of texts, grammatical and presentational features (text level).

TOTAL

8

These two writing assignments are linked to the theme of 'cats'.

The Longer Writing Test

- You should spend about 45 minutes on this.
- There are 30 marks available.

Imagine you were able to live for a day inside the body of an animal of your choice. Describe what life would be like.

In your answer you should:
- choose any animal you think appropriate;
- consider what the rest of the world would appear to be like from its point of view – shape, size, etc.;
- write about some of the situations which occurred and how you reacted to them.

Planning

Before you start writing, use the format on this page to help you to write notes. Allow time to read your work and check your use of language before you finish.

Animal and its characteristics	Animal and its habits
What would the world be like from its point of view?	**What senses would be appealed to?** What would it feel like? What would you hear and smell?
What situations would arise?	**How would you get out of them?**

The Shorter Writing Test

- You should spend about 30 minutes on this.
- There are 20 marks available.

Many bird-lovers hate cats because they say they are responsible for the decline of the bird populations in their gardens. They say they should be killed off. Write a letter to a newspaper to argue for or against this point of view.

- You should write only four paragraphs to explain your point of view, give your evidence and argue your case.
- Remember to use the appropriate letter format.

Planning

Before you start writing, use the format on this page to help you to write notes. Allow time to read your work and check your use of language before you finish.

How will you open your letter?	First paragraph: a direct statement of how you feel and why
Second paragraph: seeing the other point of view	Third paragraph: the evidence for your point of view
Fourth paragraph: any solutions to the problem	How will you close your letter?

Preparing for the Shakespeare Test

There's only one way to prepare for answering questions on a Shakespeare play – read the play! Most film and video productions are only versions of the original play so you may not get a true flavour of the original.

Shakespeare plays are not easy for us, mostly because of their language, but going to see one at the theatre will prove that they are really easy to understand as the characters think and behave in exactly the same ways as people today, four hundred years later.

Pick one of the two plays and answer the question on it.

In your test, you will be asked to deal with one aspect of the play you have studied in relation to one or two scenes, but you must also be prepared to show your knowledge of the rest of the play by putting certain aspects of the play into context, saying what has happened before and if anything has changed, and outlining what will happen later in the play.

The questions in this book give you a flavour of the kinds of questions you could find in your final tests. You will have dealt with most aspects of the play in school – character, plot and Shakespeare's language. Even if the question in front of you on the day looks different from any question you have dealt with in school, don't panic! You will have the information you need if you stop and think.

This section of your assessment differs from the others because you can prepare for this. You know what you will get, to a certain extent. You will not be allowed to take the text into the test; you need to rely on your memory and understanding of the work you have done in Year 9.

Remember: Do not write everything you know about the play – you are not being tested on how good your memory is – and answer the question you have been set, not the one you want to be set!

Strategies for the Shakespeare Test

- Draft your answer before you finally write it.

- Take time to think about what information you need from the scene printed for you.

- Spend at least 15 minutes reading the scene you have chosen carefully.

- Do not be afraid to underline or circle important quotations. Write notes in the margin as you go along.

- Use the helpful pointers given to you on the question paper and write notes on each section. Prove each of your points with a brief quotation.

- Take each of these pointers in turn and think about how to join them together as paragraphs later on. You could even number them in your notes, just to ensure that you do not miss any out.

- Do not write out huge sections from the play. The examiner wants to know what and how you write – not how Shakespeare did!

It is important that you time yourself effectively. You need to pace yourself. You have time to read and annotate the scene printed for you and time to draft and write your answer. You will not be given extra time.

You are being assessed in this section on your knowledge and awareness of the Shakespeare play you have studied – its plot, ideas, the characters and why they behave in the way that they do, the language and even the staging of the scene. But remember, you will also have to write clearly to communicate these ideas. Hence, marks are allocated for use of appropriate style, clarity and organisation of writing, spelling, grammar and punctuation. Your handwriting is also important. Make sure you leave enough time to check your work.

You can use the checklist on page 35 to help you to ensure that you include all these features in your answer.

Reading and Understanding

You should spend about 45 minutes on this section.

> Act 1 Scene 1
>
> Act 2 Scene 3
>
> **If you were acting in a performance of these scenes from 'As You Like It', what would you have to ensure the audience knew and understood about the characters and themes so that they could appreciate the rest of the play?**
>
> Support your ideas by referring to the extracts that are printed on the following pages.
>
> Before you write, you should base your answer on:
>
> - What the characters say.
> - What the characters do.
> - What others do to them.
> - What happens on the stage.
> - What impression you want the audience to have.
>
> Read the task again before you begin to write your answer.
>
> **Maximum mark: 18**

EXAMINER'S TIPS

Remind yourself about the following points:
- Set the scenes in the context of the rest of the play.
- The play begins by setting up a conflict between two brothers that will eventually lead to Orlando fighting with the wrestler Charles and being seen by Rosalind who falls in love with him.
- The danger he faces from his vengeful brother after the match means that he will also have to seek exile in the Forest of Arden.
- There, the romance between the lovers can develop.
- Many other characters are also seeking exile there. The Forest of Arden will heal them (in the way of pastoral literature) and teach them lessons so that they can be reconciled.

Planning sheet

Use this planning sheet to help you to collect material from the scenes and comment upon it.

- What the characters say

- What the characters do

CHARACTERS, THEMES, ISSUES

- Issues in the play

- Themes

- Proof from the text

Act 1 Scene 1

As You Like It

Orchard of Oliver's house.

Enter ORLANDO and ADAM

ORLANDO   As I remember, Adam, it was upon this fashion bequeathed me by will but poor a thousand crowns, and, as thou sayest, charged my brother, on his blessing, to breed me well: and there begins my sadness. My brother Jaques he keeps at school, and report speaks goldenly of his profit: for my part, he keeps me rustically at home, or, to speak more properly, stays me here at home unkept; for call you that keeping for a gentleman of my birth, that differs not from the stalling of an ox? His horses are bred better; for, besides that they are fair with their feeding, they are taught their manage, and to that end riders dearly hired: but I, his brother, gain nothing under him but growth; for the which his animals on his dunghills are as much bound to him as I. Besides this nothing that he so plentifully gives me, the something that nature gave me his countenance seems to take from me: he lets me feed with his hinds, bars me the place of a brother, and, as much as in him lies, mines my gentility with my education. This is it, Adam, that grieves me; and the spirit of my father, which I think is within me, begins to mutiny against this servitude: I will no longer endure it, though yet I know no wise remedy how to avoid it.

ADAM   Yonder comes my master, your brother.

ORLANDO   Go apart, Adam, and thou shalt hear how he will shake me up.

Enter OLIVER

OLIVER   Now, sir! what make you here?

ORLANDO   Nothing: I am not taught to make anything.

OLIVER   What mar you then, sir?

ORLANDO   Marry, sir, I am helping you to mar that which God made, a poor unworthy brother of yours, with idleness.

OLIVER   Marry, sir, be better employed, and be naught awhile.

ORLANDO   Shall I keep your hogs and eat husks with them? What prodigal portion have I spent, that I should come to such penury?

OLIVER   Know you where you are, sir?

ORLANDO   O, sir, very well; here in your orchard.

OLIVER   Know you before whom, sir?

ORLANDO	Ay, better than him I am before knows me. I know you are my eldest brother; and, in the gentle condition of blood, you should so know me. The courtesy of nations allows you my better, in that you are the first-born; but the same tradition takes not away my blood, were there twenty brothers betwixt us: I have as much of my father in me as you; albeit, I confess, your coming before me is nearer to his reverence.
OLIVER	*(threatening him)* What, boy!
ORLANDO	*(seizing him by the throat)* Come, come, elder brother, you are too young in this.
OLIVER	Wilt thou lay hands on me, villain?
ORLANDO	I am no villain; I am the youngest son of Sir Rowland de Boys; he was my father, and he is thrice a villain that says such a father begot villains. Wert thou not my brother, I would not take this hand from thy throat till this other had pulled out thy tongue for saying so: thou hast railed on thyself.

Act 2 Scene 3

As You Like It

Before OLIVER'S house.

Enter ORLANDO and ADAM, meeting

ORLANDO   Who's there?

ADAM   What, my young master? O, my gentle master!
O my sweet master! O you memory
Of old Sir Rowland! Why, what make you here?
Why are you virtuous? Why do people love you?
And wherefore are you gentle, strong and valiant?
Why would you be so fond to overcome
The bonny prizer of the humorous duke?
Your praise is come too swiftly home before you.
Know you not, master, to some kind of men
Their graces serve them but as enemies?
No more do yours: your virtues, gentle master,
Are sanctified and holy traitors to you.
O, what a world is this, when what is comely
Envenoms him that bears it!

ORLANDO   Why, what's the matter?

ADAM   O unhappy youth!
Come not within these doors; within this roof
The enemy of all your graces lives:
Your brother–no, no brother; yet the son –
Yet not the son, I will not call him son
Of him I was about to call his father –
Hath heard your praises, and this night he means
To burn the lodging where you use to lie
And you within it: if he fail of that,
He will have other means to cut you off.
I overheard him and his practices.
This is no place; this house is but a butchery:
Abhor it, fear it, do not enter it.

ORLANDO   Why, whither, Adam, wouldst thou have me go?

ADAM   No matter whither, so you come not here.

ORLANDO   What, wouldst thou have me go and beg my food?
Or with a base and boisterous sword enforce
A thievish living on the common road?
This I must do, or know not what to do:
Yet this I will not do, do how I can;
I rather will subject me to the malice
Of a diverted blood and bloody brother.

ADAM

But do not so. I have five hundred crowns,
The thrifty hire I saved under your father,
Which I did store to be my foster-nurse
When service should in my old limbs lie lame
And unregarded age in corners thrown:
Take that, and He that doth the ravens feed,
Yea, providently caters for the sparrow,
Be comfort to my age! Here is the gold;
And all this I give you. Let me be your servant:
Though I look old, yet I am strong and lusty;
For in my youth I never did apply
Hot and rebellious liquors in my blood,
Nor did not with unbashful forehead woo
The means of weakness and debility;
Therefore my age is as a lusty winter,
Frosty, but kindly: let me go with you;
I'll do the service of a younger man
In all your business and necessities.

ORLANDO

O good old man, how well in thee appears
The constant service of the antique world,
When service sweat for duty, not for meed!
Thou art not for the fashion of these times,
Where none will sweat but for promotion,
And having that, do choke their service up
Even with the having: it is not so with thee.
But, poor old man, thou prunest a rotten tree,
That cannot so much as a blossom yield
In lieu of all thy pains and husbandry
But come thy ways; we'll go along together,
And ere we have thy youthful wages spent,
We'll light upon some settled low content.

Reading and Understanding

You should spend about 45 minutes on this section.

Act 3 Scene 2

Act 3 Scene 5

If you were playing Juliet what aspects of her character would you develop in these scenes? How far would Shakespeare's language help you to do this?

Support your ideas by referring to the extracts that are printed on the following pages.

Before you write, you should base your answer on:

- What the characters say.

- What the characters do.

- What others do to them.

- What happens on the stage.

- What impression you want the audience to have.

Read the task again before you begin to write your answer.

Maximum mark: 18

EXAMINER'S TIPS

Remind yourself about the following points:

- Set the scenes in the context of the rest of the play – the feud between the families; how the lovers meet; the problem they cause; how Romeo gets into the fight with Tybalt; how Tybalt dies and how this leads to Romeo and Juliet planning to escape; how this finally happens and why.
- The killing is to start the events that will lead to the tragedy in the end.
- The stresses related to what will happen because of the killing will develop Juliet's character and make her seem no longer an innocent girl but very 'grown up'.
- Juliet is very young (13) at the start of the play, but she rapidly matures.
- Shakespeare's language reflects this – from the dreamy 'Romeo, Romeo …' to the ultimate sacrifice for love at the end when she kills herself.
- Shakespeare is using irony – the audience knows something but characters on stage do not and this leads to interest and the audience becoming more interested.

Planning sheet

Use this planning sheet to help you to collect material from the scenes and comment upon it.

JULIET			
What she says	How she says it	What she does	What others say about her

Act 3 Scene 2

Romeo and Juliet

JULIET   O, here comes my nurse,
And she brings news; and every tongue that speaks
But Romeo's name speaks heavenly eloquence.

Enter Nurse, with the ladder of cords

Now, nurse, what news? What hast thou there? the cords
That Romeo bid thee fetch?

NURSE   Ay, ay, the cords.

Throws them down

JULIET   Ay me! what news? why dost thou wring thy hands?

NURSE   Ah, well-a-day! he's dead, he's dead, he's dead!
We are undone, lady, we are undone!
Alack the day! he's gone, he's kill'd, he's dead!

JULIET   Can heaven be so envious?

NURSE   Romeo can,
Though heaven cannot: O Romeo, Romeo!
Who ever would have thought it? Romeo!

JULIET   What devil art thou, that dost torment me thus?
This torture should be roared in dismal hell.
Hath Romeo slain himself? say thou but 'I,'
And that bare vowel 'I' shall poison more
Than the death-darting eye of cockatrice:
I am not I, if there be such an I;
Or those eyes shut, that make thee answer 'I.'
If he be slain, say 'I'; or if not, no:
Brief sounds determine of my weal or woe.

NURSE   I saw the wound, I saw it with mine eyes,
(God save the mark!), here on his manly breast:
A piteous corse, a bloody piteous corse;
Pale, pale as ashes, all bedaub'd in blood,
All in gore-blood; I sounded at the sight.

JULIET   O, break, my heart! poor bankrupt, break at once!
To prison, eyes, ne'er look on liberty!
Vile earth, to earth resign; end motion here;
And thou and Romeo press one heavy bier!

NURSE   O Tybalt, Tybalt, the best friend I had!
O courteous Tybalt! honest gentleman!
That ever I should live to see thee dead!

JULIET	What storm is this that blows so contrary?
	Is Romeo slaughter'd, and is Tybalt dead?
	My dear-loved cousin, and my dearer lord?
	Then, dreadful trumpet, sound the general doom!
	For who is living, if those two are gone?

NURSE   Tybalt is gone, and Romeo banished;
Romeo that kill'd him, he is banished.

JULIET   O God! did Romeo's hand shed Tybalt's blood?

NURSE   It did, it did; alas the day, it did!

JULIET   O serpent heart, hid with a flowering face!
Did ever dragon keep so fair a cave?
Beautiful tyrant! fiend angelical!
Dove-feather'd raven! wolvish-ravening lamb!
Despised substance of divinest show!
Just opposite to what thou justly seem'st,
A damned saint, an honourable villain!
O nature, what hadst thou to do in hell,
When thou didst bower the spirit of a fiend
In moral paradise of such sweet flesh?
Was ever book containing such vile matter
So fairly bound? O that deceit should dwell
In such a gorgeous palace!

NURSE   There's no trust,
No faith, no honesty in men; all perjured,
All forsworn, all naught, all dissemblers.
Ah, where's my man? Give me some aqua vitae:
These griefs, these woes, these sorrows make me old.
Shame come to Romeo!

JULIET   Blister'd be thy tongue
For such a wish! he was not born to shame:
Upon his brow shame is ashamed to sit;
For 'tis a throne where honour may be crown'd
Sole monarch of the universal earth.
O, what a beast was I to chide at him!

NURSE   Will you speak well of him that kill'd your cousin?

Act 3 Scene 5

Romeo and Juliet

JULIET	O fortune, fortune! all men call thee fickle: If thou art fickle, what dost thou with him. That is renown'd for faith? Be fickle, fortune; For then, I hope, thou wilt not keep him long, But send him back.
LADY CAPULET	[Within] Ho, daughter! are you up?
JULIET	Who is't that calls? It is my lady mother. Is she not down so late, or up so early? What unaccustomed cause procures her hither?
	Enter LADY CAPULET
LADY CAPULET	Why, how now, Juliet!
JULIET	Madam, I am not well.
LADY CAPULET	Evermore weeping for your cousin's death? What, wilt thou wash him from his grave with tears? An if thou couldst, thou couldst not make him live; Therefore, have done: some grief shows much of love; But much of grief shows still some want of wit.
JULIET	Yet let me weep for such a feeling loss.
LADY CAPULET	So shall you feel the loss, but not the friend Which you weep for.
JULIET	Feeling so the loss, Cannot choose but ever weep the friend.
LADY CAPULET	Well, girl, thou weep'st not so much for his death, As that the villain lives which slaughter'd him.
JULIET	What villain madam?
LADY CAPULET	That same villain, Romeo.
JULIET	[Aside] Villain and he be many miles asunder, – God Pardon him! I do, with all my heart; And yet no man like he doth grieve my heart.
LADY CAPULET	That is, because the traitor murderer lives.
JULIET	Ay, madam, from the reach of these my hands: Would none but I might venge my cousin's death!

LADY CAPULET	We will have vengeance for it, fear thou not:
	Then weep no more. I'll send to one in Mantua,
	Where that same banish'd runagate doth live,
	Shall give him such an unaccustomed dram,
	That he shall soon keep Tybalt company:
	And then, I hope, thou wilt be satisfied.
JULIET	Indeed, I never shall be satisfied
	With Romeo, till I behold him – dead –
	Is my poor heart for a kinsman vex'd.
	Madam, if you could find out but a man
	To bear a poison, I would temper it;
	That Romeo should, upon receipt thereof,
	Soon sleep in quiet. O, how my heart abhors
	To hear him named, and cannot come to him.
	To wreak the love I bore my cousin
	Upon his body that slaughter'd him!
LADY CAPULET	Find thou the means, and I'll find such a man.
	But now I'll tell thee joyful tidings, girl.
JULIET	And joy comes well in such a needy time:
	What are they, I beseech your ladyship?
LADY CAPULET	Well, well, thou hast a careful father, child;
	One who, to put thee from thy heaviness,
	Hath sorted out a sudden day of joy,
	That thou expects not nor I looked not for.
JULIET	Madam, in happy time, what day is that?
LADY CAPULET	Marry, my child, early next Thursday morn,
	The gallant, young and noble gentleman,
	The County Paris, at Saint Peter's Church,
	Shall happily make thee there a joyful bride.
JULIET	Now, by Saint Peter's Church and Peter too,
	He shall not make me there a joyful bride.
	I wonder at this haste; that I must wed
	Ere he, that should be husband, comes to woo.
	I pray you, tell my lord and father, madam,
	I will not marry yet; and, when I do, I swear,
	It shall be Romeo, whom you know I hate,
	Rather than Paris. These are news indeed!
LADY CAPULET	Here comes your father; tell him so yourself,
	And see how he will take it at your hands.

Answers

Fiction (*The Daydreamer*)

1. The problem emerges because the boy 'inside' the cat is not aware of the way animals are expected to react in their environment. He still thinks as a human even though he is 'inside' the cat.
Presumably, the cat which Peter has 'taken over' is an old cat, 'He's seventeen if he's a day'; hence the 'Grandad' references. He would normally give way to the younger black cat. They both challenge each other but the black cat is confident – and would rightly be so if he were fighting a 'normal cat'. Compared to Peter he is 'twice his size' – much stronger.
The animals think the situation is amusing and the black cat stays to 'enjoy' the fight. He does give Peter the opportunity to back down. The other cats stand around and watch – expecting Peter to be defeated.
When the black cat strikes, Peter uses his human reasoning to assess the situation. The cat will be balanced on three legs at a certain time and hence he can be attacked with surprise. The black cat has strength and youth to fight with. Peter is able to launch himself and push the cat from the wall by catching him off-balance. He behaves in an 'un-cat-like' way and this ensures him success. This is seen as 'unfair' tactics by the other cat. **2 marks**

2. The black cat talks in the language of gangster stories, '"Hey puss," he hissed …". His speech is characterised by threat and insult to give the reader another glimpse into the world of cats. Here we have a rough, tough street-wise cat against the 'softer' version in Peter. Peter tries to keep his voice calm but his words come out as a cat hiss, 'You don't take ssshort cutsss here'. **2 marks**

3. 'delight to walk on four soft white paws'
'see his whiskers springing out from the sides of his face'
'he felt his tail curling behind him'
There are others. **2 marks**

4.

1	2	3	4	5
E	B	A	D	C

2 marks

5. The opening paragraph immediately gives us a feeling of what it might be like to be a cat. The writer appeals to the senses, 'walk on four soft white paws' – he realises the animal walks in a different way. He can 'see his whiskers' out of the side of his face – these are a large and important physical feature to cats; he 'felt his tail curling behind him'; his 'tread was light' and the purr emerges from him as a sense of pleasure.
The writer also uses carefully chosen language to describe the features – the softness of the tread of the cat suggesting caution, the whiskers 'springing' suggesting life, the tail 'curling' reinforcing the idea that a cat's tail is constantly moving in a smooth way; the fur is comfortable like 'old woollen jumpers'. Cats give us the impression as they move of being completely at ease with their bodies and the environment.
Peter is now more awake at night – cats are more nocturnal – and he does not feel the cold. He moves like a cat, 'padded soundlessly', and can see and feel more sensitively as a cat – 'feel every vibration of the night air on his whiskers'. He can jump very high up the wall and is aware of all the animal happenings in the environment – the human aspects of the world no longer matter to him.
When he first meets the black cat he is surprised by his feelings of wanting to protect his territory and by his aggression towards the animal. He has no previous knowledge of how animals behave in this environment. When he communicates his words come 'out in a hiss' suggesting the cat's aggression. He 'arched his back and upended his fur' – an instinctive reaction in a cat to 'make himself look big'.
Later, following his cat-like characteristics, he picks the warmest spot to lie – the radiator shelf – and plans to move to the warmth of the bed later. He describes a typical cat-like pose – the paw dangling, the 'head cushioned on one paw'.
He describes the day in the life of a cat – 'Dozing, lapping a saucer of milk, dozing again' and ends the extract in front of the fire being stroked. **4 marks**

Non-Fiction (*Having Kittens?*)

6. 'Do all you can to make your kitten comfortable'. **1 mark**

7. Open windows – the kitten could fall out as he has probably not had any experience of them before.
Breakages – kittens tend to break things in their exuberance, so valuables need to be kept out of the way. **2 marks**

8. a) You need to make a particular sound or use a name when talking to your new pet so they can associate the sound with routines during their day: 'your kitten can associate with feeding and play time'.
b) You should place the kitten *gently* in his litter tray after every meal so that he does not associate this part of his ritual as something being forced upon him. If this was the case he would probably become afraid and run away, so defeating the object of placing him there. **2 marks**

9. Instructions tend to use the imperative, command voice, 'explain … introduce … Do … Don't …'
They use the second person 'you' pronoun.
Instructions mostly use the present tense and follow a logical sequence. **2 marks**

10. The booklet aims to present information as simply and effectively as possible. The information is practical and based on experience.
The audience will be one that may not know the language and subject matter – if they have never had a kitten before.
The pages provide a mix of text, headings and coloured boxes to make its impact – emotional and factual. The picture of the cat is very 'appealing'.
The language used is direct and uses the second person 'you' to talk direct to the audience. It is almost like having a conversation. Straight away, it puts the situation into a personal context by making the reader imagine what the situation of moving into a new house would be like for him/her.
The basic 'Do's' and 'Don't's are given succinctly, using italics to make them stand out. The instructions use the imperative (command) tone. All the advice is very practical – even down to warning owners about the wearing of rubber gloves.
The 'paws for thought' box contains key points.
All through the booklet, sub-headings are used so that the reader can judge which parts of the text are most relevant to them. Different typefaces and sizes are used for titles, and the colour blue is used. In all it is about clarity, using simple language and a personal response to the reader.   **5 marks**

Poetry (Cat)

11. Any of the following: 'a-purr'; 'As o'er your fur'; ''neath many an arch'.   **1 mark**

12. 'exquisite', 'luxurious' and 'imperial' suggest that the cat is from a royal background.   **1 mark**

13. *With tail erect and pompous march* suggests that the cat is aloof and is confident in the way she walks (her tail); she walks in a proud 'pompous' way – she is at home in this environment and is respected, i.e. *The proudest puss that ever trod.* **2 marks**

14. The image
my wondering eye
Salutes a more imperial moon
Throned in a more resplendent sky
suggests a regal view. 'Salutes' suggests a quick looking up at the sky – a look of recognition as in a military salute. The moon seems 'imperial' – royal in some way and is like a royal personage seated on a throne in the sky – almost a goddess. **2 marks**

15.   **2 marks**

Subject	Answer – verse
The poet wonders what mystery lies behind the eyes of the cat.	2
The poet feels he is in a warmer place with an exotic moon.	4
The poet strokes the cat as she sleeps.	1
The cat is proud and honoured in this society.	6
The poet suddenly feels as if he has been transported to an ancient time with incense and palaces.	3
The poet imagines the cat in an ancient palace at night.	7
The poet feels he is the cat following a woman in ancient times.	5

National Curriculum Levels

Score	Criteria	NC Level
31–32	Exceptional answer	7+
24–30	Well above average answer	7
16–23	Above average answer	6
9–15	Average or below average answer	5
1–8	Well below average answer	4 or below

Answers

Writing Test

This test is marked for overall impression – there is not a set of correct points which should be incorporated. Both content and how the content is communicated – style, grammar, punctuation, accuracy – are considered.

However, there is a set of marking criteria which needs to be considered:

Does the answer:	Yes	No
communicate ideas clearly to you?		
use a suitable style for the purpose indicated in the question?		
organise the material in an appropriate way to the style?		
use paragraphs, correct grammar and punctuation?		
spell words correctly and make use of relevant words precisely?		
look neat and make reading easy?		

The Longer Writing Test – criteria for marking

Marked out of 30. Follow the sequence of these sections to build a picture of strengths and weaknesses.

Sentence structure and punctuation

Criteria	Marks	NC Level
Ideas mostly linked. Simple conjunctions such as *and* and *but* used. Simple and compound sentences. Little variation in word order; subjects and verbs repeated. Piece lacks language variety. Basic punctuation marks: full stops, capital letters, question marks used correctly.	1–2	Below 4
Construction of sentences varied: for example, use of relative clauses, *who* and *which*. Complex conjunctions used for effect: for example, *if* to suggest alternative, *because* to suggest cause and effect. Commas used correctly.	3–4	4
Variety of sentences: simple, compound, complex. Phrases and clauses used to convey interesting information. Different sentence types: questions, commands. Verbs used more creatively: *would, could, can*. Punctuation used correctly to demarcate sentences.	5–6	5
Sentences contain complex grammatical structures, to vary length and meaning. Sentences used to create deliberate effects, and punctuation supports this: bullet points, brackets, dashes.	7	6
Sentences show control and variation. Punctuation is accurate, creates deliberate effects and avoids ambiguity.	8	7+

Text structure and organisation

Criteria	Marks	NC Level
Some ideas are linked through the subject or topic. Use of some paragraphs, but not always accurate. Ideas tend to be listed and not grouped appropriately.	1–2	Below 4
Paragraphs are used. They open with a topic sentence and contain examples to develop and back up the thesis. Ideas are not well developed.	3–4	4
Some logical sequence of paragraphs to support the argument or idea. The writer introduces and concludes the text. Paragraphs of different lengths are deliberately used for persuasion or development.	5–6	5
Content is fairly detailed and well organised. Sophisticated connectives: for example, for relationships (*on the other hand*). Topic sentences are used in the most effective places. Introductory paragraph directs the thought process and purpose. Conclusion rounds off ideas.	7	6
Paragraphs are varied and the writer is obviously in control of his or her ideas. Structure held together by sophisticated use of connectives. Paragraphs varied in structure to create impact.	8	7+

Composition and effect

Criteria	Marks	NC Level
Written form appropriate and shows some awareness of the reader. Content mainly relevant.	1–3	Below 4
The form is used in a lively and correct way. The writer is aware that he or she has to interest the reader. Reasons given to support views, or details to reinforce purpose.	4–6	4
Detailed attention given to the subject in an appropriate style for the purpose of the writing. Reasons or details are clear and interest the reader. Style is controlled and fairly convincing; viewpoint is clear.	7–9	5
Text is structured effectively and the style is appropriate to purpose. Writer uses details persuasively. Writer's viewpoint is consistent throughout.	10–12	6
Tone and content of the written piece are carefully controlled and sustained. Written piece is of interest to the reader. Content is carefully and relevantly selected to support purpose of text.	13–14	7+

Checklist
Assessing Written Expression

Use these charts below to check your child's work. They give an indication of the level achieved.

Level 4	Yes	No
Ideas clearly expressed		
Paragraphs – organised ideas		
Punctuation of separate sentences generally accurate		
Spelling of simple words accurate		
Handwriting clear and legible		

Level 5	Yes	No
Ideas clearly expressed		
Wide vocabulary, precise use of words		
Simple and complex sentences used – ordered into paragraphs		
Variety of punctuation – apostrophes and commas used correctly		
Spelling of words – complex regular patterns – accurate		
Handwriting – clear, legible, fluent		

Level 6	Yes	No
Ideas clearly expressed with a sense of purpose		
A varied vocabulary used – appropriate language expressed in simple and complex sentences – good paragraphing		
Spelling accurate – some difficult words still incorrect		
Range of punctuation used – some more difficult forms		
Handwriting fluent and legible		

Level 7	Yes	No
Confidently expressed ideas – words chosen are appropriate		
Appropriate style is matched by appropriate language		
Accurate grammar and punctuation – being consciously used for effect		
Correct paragraphing and punctuation		
Correct spelling of irregular words		
Handwriting consistently fluent and legible		

The Shorter Writing Test – criteria for marking

Marked out of 20. Follow the sequence of these sections to build a picture of strengths and weaknesses.

Sentence structure, punctuation and text organisation

Criteria	Marks	NC Level
A range of nouns and adjectives is used, but no real variety. Little evidence of choosing words for meaning and effect. Not using vocabulary precisely to enhance meaning. Ideas and phrases linked by simple conjunctions; mainly simple or compound sentences. Writer does not vary word order or sentence constructions. Basic punctuation and capital letters are used to demarcate sentences in a simple paragraph structure.	1–2	4
Attempt to use vocabulary to create some effects and interest the reader. Adjectives and adverbs begin to add detail to descriptions. Choice of verbs becoming more accurate. Writer uses varied sentences (relative clauses use *who* and *which* appropriately). Verb tenses and pronouns used consistently. More sophisticated forms of punctuation: for example, commas used correctly. Paragraphs show that the author is selecting detail in a planned way.	3–4	5
Word choice is appropriate to the form of writing and serves to advance the purpose of the writer. Verbs, adjectives and adverbs are used to add to the effects required. More complex and compound sentences used. Writer uses phrases and clauses to add detail and information. The meaning in sentences is more precise through the correct use of pronouns, tenses and qualifying adverbs. Paragraphs are used and material in them is sequenced effectively.	5	6
A full range of vocabulary is used from simple to the most complicated in order to achieve the required effects and interest the reader. Writer is aware of how to manipulate language through wordplay and patterning. The tone and authorial stance are assisted by the consistent use of adjectives and adverbs. The writer manipulates the length and focus of sentences to achieve the required effect. Writer is aware of how grammatical structures can be used to achieve these effects. Punctuation varied and used correctly. Paragraphs are varied in length and structure to contribute effectively to the piece of writing as a whole.	6	7+

Composition and effect

Criteria	Marks	NC Level
The form of writing shows some awareness of the reader, audience and purpose. Writer uses some stylistic features to achieve an effect. Content chosen is mostly relevant.	1–3	4
Text has a sense of purpose relevant to the form used and aims to interest the reader. Writer is aware of stylistic devices such as patterning and repetition to achieve particular effects. The topic is covered with relevant detail, but writing tends not to be original. Clear sense of audience and purpose. Consistent and persuasive. Style and tone of writing appeal to reader. Appropriate vocabulary.	4–6	5
Writer shows a secure grasp of the form of writing, establishing purpose and sense of context for reader. Concepts such as setting and character are developed. Stylistic devices are used to communicate meaning. Narration and description are used together but writer reflects upon them to establish authorial stance.	7–9	6
Text is carefully written and form matches purpose. It maintains interest of reader, so achieving its aim. Stylistic effects and relevant details are used confidently to achieve required viewpoint. Writer is aware of how to balance information, description and explanation.	10	7

Spelling

Criteria	Marks	NC Level
The spelling of simple and common words of more than one syllable is usually correct.	1	4
The spelling of words containing complex regular patterns is usually accurate.	2	5
Most spelling is correct.	3	6
Nearly all spelling is correct.	4	7

Pupil Checklist
Important features in your answer

Features to consider	Yes	No
Paragraphs Is my work divided into paragraphs so that the examiner can see when I stop writing about one aspect and start writing about another? (This is an important stylistic feature and helps you communicate your message clearly to the examiner.)		
Quotations Are my quotations too long? Have I used quotation marks? Have I started big quotations on a new line? Have I written my quotations on lines as in the text? Have I introduced my quotations by using a colon (:)?		
Style Is my writing too chatty? Am I writing in an appropriate style? Have I written in complete sentences? Is my handwriting clear and neat?		
Length (The answer booklet you will be given in the test is A4 in size. If you use any pages for planning, just draw a line through these.) Have I written between 3 and 4 sides on A4 paper for my answer?		

As You Like It: Reading and Understanding

- This question tests understanding of character, themes, language and dramatic conventions.
- The answer will be assessed only for understanding of the play and for how pupils respond to its literary merits. It will not be assessed for written expression.
- There are 18 marks available for this section of the test.
- Follow the sequence of the guidelines below to build a picture of strengths and weaknesses. Use the Key Points on page 37 to award marks.

Criteria for marking	NC Levels
Well below average	
Only a few simple facts from the play about character and plot. Story of extract is retold. The writer does not attempt to adopt the point of view or the approach required.	Below 4
Below average	
Shows some awareness of character reactions. Some comparison of the two extracts. Comments mostly at level of the plot. Requested point of view not sustained although some attempt is made. Some relevant quotation made.	4
Average	
Commentary given shows some understanding. Character reactions understood. Comparison of two passages. No development of points made. Some awareness of how actors behave within dramatic conventions. References supported by quotations.	4/5
Average/above average	
More commentary with reference to characters on stage and how the drama works. Real comparison of the two extracts. Explores the way characters could behave to make feelings clear, etc. Some knowledge of Shakespeare's use of language and how this is working to achieve his aims. Direct quotation given.	5
Above average	
Concentration on the focus of the question. Character reactions explained in terms of the play and the dramatic conventions. Understanding of the tone and role expected by the question. Comments justified by relevant reference to texts. Comparison between passages evident.	6
Well above average	
Interpretation of the role of characters and the relationship to central themes. Comparison of two extracts using comparative quotations. Exploration of the ways actors could show reactions. Language effects appreciated. Precisely selected and timely quotation.	7 and above

As You Like It: Key Points

Two marks for each key point

1. The play deals with major conflicts between the two pairs of brothers: Oliver and Orlando, and Duke Frederick and Duke Senior. Both end in exile and in the Forest of Arden. Orlando is the younger brother and so did not inherit his father's property, but his rights are being taken from him. In the case of the Duke, it is the *younger* brother who is usurping the rights of the *elder* brother. In Shakespeare's time this would be seen as a sin.

2. In this opening scene, Shakespeare begins to develop a theme common to Elizabethan pastoral literature: 'gentleness' or what it means to have those gentlemanly virtues – nobility and a virtuous nature. Elizabethans were interested in whether these qualities could be achieved/learned or whether someone had to be born with them. Orlando seems to be asking this question and 'rustic' characters in the Forest of Arden are there to examine this idea.

3. When Oliver enters, Orlando has had enough of the situation and decides to fight back. He tells him that "the spirit of my father, which I think is within me, begins to mutiny against this servitude." The two brothers argue. Orlando grabs Oliver and demands that he receive the education and the treatment due him or else he wants the thousand crowns to which he is entitled to, according to their father's will.

4. Oliver's own cruel and villainous character is explained in Orlando's opening speech – his father's will has been ignored. Later, Oliver coldly tells Adam, the old and faithful family servant, to leave the room. He lies to Charles, a professional wrestler, and encourages him to harm, if not kill, Orlando. The Duke's wrestler Charles has heard that Orlando intends to come in disguise and "try a fall" with him. Later, Oliver shows his true intent: "I had as lief thou didst break his neck as his finger … I hope I shall see an end of him; for my soul — yet I know not why — hates nothing more than he."

5. The second scene reveals more about Oliver's evil character. When Orlando meets Adam, returning home after the wrestling match, Adam tells him that as he has won, Oliver is plotting to burn down Orlando's sleeping quarters that very night. "Abhor it," Adam warns, "fear it, do not enter it". Oliver will try to murder Orlando by some other means if this does not work. He warns Orlando to leave immediately and offers him his life's savings of five hundred crowns.

6. Adam is very much seen as a 'good' character – the epitome of the faithful servant – kind, devoted and thoughtful to the extreme for his master, in contrast with Duke Frederick who may be more educated but is cruel and self-seeking. Orlando also treats him kindly and respects him, even if he is his servant.

7. These conflicts and evil actions between brothers contrast with the idyllic, 'pastoral' atmosphere in the Forest of Arden – almost like the world of the fairy tale of Robin Hood, to which we will be introduced soon and where most of the action takes place. Those wounded by life at court are seeking the restorative powers of the country.

8. The scenes also focus on the matter of city life versus country living, a theme throughout the play and something key to Elizabethan thinking. Orlando points out that he is being kept "rustically at home". He is not going away to learn how to be a gentleman. Later, he decides to leave his pastoral home to seek his fortune elsewhere. Later this theme is discussed by Jaques in his famous "All the world's a stage" speech (Act 2, Scene 7) and in the scenes between Touchstone, the fool, and Corin, the country shepherd (Act 3, Scene 2). Much of the debate of the play will be about the corrupt nature of so-called civilised life. People have fled from the forest to escape this and the 'natural' people of the forest do not have such sins.

9. Orlando's character is introduced to us. He is portrayed to us as someone fairly innocent of the world and in his actions quite inexperienced. This would be because he has not been given the education of a gentleman. He is obviously quick to anger and becomes violent with his brother but treats his old servant with respect and loyalty – unlike his brother. He is determined, brave and courageous. Shakespeare wants us to see him 'grow up' in the forest. Even his own brother says: "he's gentle, never schooled and yet learned, full of noble device, of all sorts enchantingly beloved…" His reaction to his servant and the offer of money show this.

Romeo and Juliet: **Reading and Understanding**

- The question will test understanding of character, themes, language and dramatic conventions.

- The answer will be assessed only for understanding of the play and for how pupils respond to its literary merits. It will not be assessed for written expression.

- There are **18** marks available for this section of the test.

- Follow the sequence of the guidelines below to build a picture of strengths and weaknesses. Use the Key Points on page 40 to award marks.

Criteria for marking	NC Levels
Well below average	
Only a few simple facts from the play about character and plot. Story of extract is retold. The writer does not attempt to adopt the point of view or the approach required.	Below 4
Below average	
Shows some awareness of character reactions. Some comparison of the two extracts. Comments mostly at level of the plot. Requested point of view not sustained although some attempt is made. Some relevant quotation made.	4
Average	
Commentary given showing some understanding. Character reactions understood. Comparison of two passages. No development of points made. Some awareness of how actors behave within dramatic conventions. References supported by quotations.	4/5
Average/above average	
More commentary with reference to characters on stage and how the drama works. Real comparison of the two extracts. Explores the way characters could behave to make feelings clear, etc. Some knowledge of Shakespeare's use of language and how this is working to achieve his aims. Direct quotation given.	5
Above average	
Concentration on the focus of the question. Character reactions explained in terms of the play and the dramatic conventions. Understanding of the tone and role expected by the question. Comments justified by relevant reference to texts. Comparison between passages evident.	6
Well above average	
Interpretation of the role of characters and the relationship to central themes. Comparison of two extracts using comparative quotations. Exploration of the ways actors could show reactions. Language effects appreciated. Precisely selected and timely quotation.	7 and above

Romeo and Juliet: Key Points

Two marks for each key point

1. Earlier in the play, Romeo has accidentally killed Tybalt and the Montague–Capulet feud is continued. Romeo is to be banished from Verona – an important plot device. The couple are now secretly married. The killing is to start the events that will lead to the tragedy in the end.

2. Juliet passes through a variety of moods in the scene as a young girl in love – elation, puzzlement, fear, passion. The stresses related to what will happen now will develop her character and make her seem very 'grown up'.

3. She is passionate and dreamy to start with in the speech where she imagines him as "little stars", then she becomes concerned thinking him dead and then worried about the impact of Tybalt's death on their plans and happiness. She curses the nurse and praises her lover: "he was not born to shame".

4. The nurse does not tell Juliet immediately that she is mistaken – it is as if she is trying to persuade her that Romeo is all that others say he is, but Juliet will not believe this. She does doubt him to begin with: "O serpent heart, hid with a flowering face … beautiful tyrant … fiend angelical."

5. Juliet's love for Romeo is so strong that she would rather kill herself than have to marry Paris, and thus, betray Romeo and their marriage together. This notion of what Juliet is willing to do for love comes up again, as it did before, when she says "I'll no longer be a Capulet". Even though Romeo has killed one of her relatives Juliet keeps faith with him.

6. Juliet is brave enough to go along with the Friar's plan. She is a young, innocent girl but must also be seen as intelligent beyond her years. The friar gives Juliet a sleeping potion that will make it look as if she is dead. She knows that this will be a difficult plan to carry out, but she looks to her love for Romeo to give her the strength to follow it through.

7. Lady Capulet mistakes Juliet's tears for Romeo as grief for Tybalt's death – again ironic for the audience and something linked the appearance and reality theme. Juliet even threatens vengeance, promising to have Romeo poisoned in Mantua, "O how my heart abhors to hear him named". Juliet is becoming cleverer in what she is doing to be with her lover – lying to her mother, "I swear/It shall be Romeo, whom you know I hate …", being someone she really is not – but fate will mean that they both die. Juliet shows considerable courage to defy her parents and go to Friar Lawrence.

8. Shakespeare plays with words in many of the speeches: the puns in Act 3 Scene 2 on "ay", "I" and 'eyes' in the speeches between Juliet and her nurse. Passionate language comes from raw emotion when Juliet thinks that Romeo is dead: "Vile earth, to earth resign, end motion here" – she wants to die to end her suffering.

9. Often language can develop themes such as appearance and reality: Romeo becomes "damned saint", "beautiful tyrant" showing how their situation was created out of impossibilities and opposites. Double meanings are deliberate throughout the words of Act 3 Scene 5. Lady Capulet thinks that Juliet is agreeing with her but she is meaning the opposite.

The Mark Scheme and National Curriculum Levels

READING (including marks for Shakespeare paper) – Out of 50	Minimum marks awarded	Maximum marks awarded
Below Level 4	0	9
Level 4	10	15
Level 5	16	26
Level 6	27	33
Level 7	34	50

WRITING – Out of 50	Minimum marks awarded	Maximum marks awarded
Below Level 4	0	8
Level 4	9	17
Level 5	18	26
Level 6	27	34
Level 7	35	50

AGGREGATED TOTAL – Out of 100	Minimum marks awarded	Maximum marks awarded
Below Level 4	0	18
Level 4	19	33
Level 5	34	53
Level 6	54	68
Level 7	69	100